R is for rugby

A COLLECTION OF ANECDOTES, QUOTES AND RUGBY STORIES WITH A FOREWORD BY JONATHAN DAVIES.

Compiled and Written by Iain Spragg

R is for rugby

This edition first published in the UK in 2005

By Green Umbrella

www.greenumbrella.co.uk

© Green Umbrella Publishing 2005

Publishers Jules Gammond, Tim Exell

Printed and bound in China.

ISBN 1-905009-08-9

Contents

Foreword
Jonathan Davies

Hollywood legend Richard Burton once said "rugby is a wonderful show. Dance, opera and, suddenly, the blood of a killing." The late, great comedian Spike Milligan perhaps put it more succinctly when he observed, "rugby is a game for big buggers; if you're not a big bugger, you get hurt."

Two schools of thought, maybe, but one common thread – the love of a game that is played in every corner of the globe by many millions of seemingly sane people.

Looking back, it's doubtful whether William Webb Ellis could have realised he had unwittingly invented a sport which would prove so popular and so enduring when he famously 'picked up the ball and ran with it' at Rugby School way back in 1823. He certainly would have had no idea what a source of persistent humour and comedy 'his' game would provide for players and fans alike over the years to come. 'R is for Rugby' celebrates those involved at every level of the game through the decades and the marvellously mad and indescribably insane things they do in the name of sport.

So whether you're a rugby fanatic looking for a laugh or a mere novice to the game trying to fathom just what it is that makes rugby folk tick, this book has it all. From the near-fatal case of the England player hospitalised by a gift from his French hosts and the violence-shy Communist officials who banned the game, to the less-than-fearless British and Irish Lion tourist and the thief-snatching Italian star duo, the pages that follow are a teeming treasure trove of rugby's most bizarre, painful and amusing anecdotes.

Of course, like the game itself, 'R is for Rugby' is not always for the feint-hearted or those of a nervous disposition and the excruciating tale of the All Black legend who nearly became half the man he was, or the sickening story of the Brive bar room brawl, prove you certainly have to be a little (or a lot) mad to truly embrace the game.

After all, what other sport can lay claim to a Pope and a brutal dictator, a former American president and a comic genius among its former players?

So sit back, relax and enjoy. 'Rugby is like an organised orgy', an anonymous wag once wrote. After reading this book, you'll understand why.

YOU DON'T HAVE TO BE MAD!
A TRIBUTE TO THE MEN WHO PLAY THE GAME

Chapter 1

Rugby, as the old joke goes, is a game played by men with odd-shaped balls. The men themselves come in all shapes and sizes, colours and creeds, but are all united by one alarmingly common characteristic – every single one of them is just a little bit mad.

This chapter pays tribute to these brave but barmy men from the different eras of the game and their frequent bouts of insanity and stupidity and humour. After all, without the players rugby would be a rather dull game indeed.

In the pages that follow you'll meet, amongst others, the cigarette-smoking prop who dropped a right clanger, the international forward who had an embarrassing spot of bother in the car park and the future Lions star who tragically misplaced his shorts.

And when you've read these and the other bizarre tales of players behaving badly, madly and often very sadly, you'll wonder just why they're allowed out in public without suitable adult supervision.

To paraphrase one former international who shall remain nameless, you really don't have to be that bright to be a rugby player...

Collision course...

Some players are immortalised in the annals of the game for all the right reasons – and some, sadly, for moments of sheer madness that will forever strike a chord with anyone who has finished a match with egg well and truly on their face.

Take Sale and England winger Hal Sever, who won 10 caps for his country in the 1930s, but will probably always be remembered for the unfortunate time he handed Scotland victory at Twickenham in the most comic of circumstances.

BELOW Andy Robinson, President of the RFU – Derek Morgan, Hal Sever, Tom Kemp and Clive Woodward.

With the game in the dying minutes of the second-half – and Scotland narrowly leading 18-16 – England mounted a last, desperate attack which saw Sever put clean through for what would have surely been the winning try.

But rather than race for the corner, the winger cut inside the defence and his moment of glory was cruelly snatched away as he crashed into one of the uprights and dropped the ball.

And if that was not bad enough, Scotland pounced on the loose ball and mounted a counter-attack which culminated in a try at the other end, sealing a famous victory.

Up in smoke...

Modern rugby players in the professional age are (or at least should be) finely-tuned athletes, but the same could not always be said of their amateur predecessors.

One such player was Ireland prop Phil O'Callaghan. The big forward was named in Ireland's squad for the 1975 game against a President's XV at Lansdowne Road.
The match was part of the IRFU's centenary celebrations and everyone expected a party atmosphere in Dublin.

ABOVE Big Phil O'Callaghan on the charge.

O'Callaghan started on the bench but was soon called into action. As he packed down for his first scrum, a packet of cigarettes and a lighter fell out of his pockets in full view of the crowd and his team-mates.

But rather than hang his head in shame, O'Callaghan bent down, calmly picked up the offending items up off the floor and handed them to the stunned referee.

He then politely asked the official if he'd hang onto them until half-time, because he didn't like oranges.

New ball please...

Rugby has produced plenty of acknowledged hard men in its history and everyone has their own theory on who really was the toughest of the tough.

One player, however, who would surely make anyone's top ten has to be former New Zealand number eight Wayne 'Buck' Shelford, who more than proved his hard man credentials in the All Blacks international against France in 1986.

The match, which later became known as the 'Battle of Nantes', was only Shelford's second cap and the New Zealander soon found himself at the bottom of a ruck and several pairs of indiscriminate, size 10 French boots.

Unluckily for him, one of the flying studs ripped his scrotum and his testicle was left hanging, quite literally, by a thread. But rather than leave the field, Shelford ordered the All Blacks physio to stitch the wound back up so he could carry on!

BELOW Hard man Wayne 'Buck' Shelford in quiet, relaxed mood.

"I was knocked out cold, lost a few teeth and had a few stitches down below," Shelford said after he retired. "It's a game I still can't remember – I have no memory of it whatsoever." Which for him is probably a blessing.

Genuine all rounder...

There have been many rugby players who have also excelled in other fields, but there can be few who can rival the wide-ranging achievements of Englishman Charles Burgess Fry.

Although he never won a full England cap, CB Fry (as he was more commonly known) represented the Barbarians in a first-class fixture and won 26 Test cricket caps for his country.

But that was only the tip of the iceberg. Fry also played football for England and, at one time, he was joint world record holder in the long jump.

But even as his sporting prowess diminished, Fry continued to make his mark in the wider world, working as a delegate for the League of Nations.
He was even asked to become the King of Albania, although this was one honour he declined.

ABOVE All round sportsman and cricketer Charles Burgess Fry (1872 – 1956). He represented England in athletics, cricket and soccer and also gained an Oxford blue in all three.

Flying visit...

There's nothing like a late injury to throw your pre-match preparations into disarray, as England experienced in 1930 in the hours before their international against Wales in Cardiff.

The day before the game, the England hooker Henry Rew was injured in training and the next morning it was confirmed he could not play. Cue an SOS to Bristol hooker Sam Tucker, a First World War veteran who was wounded at the Battle of the Somme, and an epic if frequently frantic journey that defied the odds.

By the time Tucker received the news of his late call-up he realised he had already missed the last train from Bristol to Cardiff that would arrive in the Welsh capital in time, so he chartered a private plane which eventually landed in a field near Cardiff.

Desperate not to miss kick-off, Tucker ran across two fields and hitched a lift from

BELOW The England team to face Wales in 1926 included the legendary Bristolian Sam Tucker (centre row, second from left).

a passing lorry which duly took him into the city. But with the minutes ticking by, and thousands of fans blocking his way, he was still not at the ground, so he collared a policeman and was escorted in record time into the stadium.

Tucker eventually made his appearance in the England dressing room just five minutes before kick-off. Fortunately for the fleet-footed Bristolian, England ran out 11-3 winners.

Car park craziness...

Many matches have been delayed, interrupted or even abandoned for bizarre reasons but there is only one to date that has been held up while a player finds his car keys.

The game in question was the 1996 Pilkington Cup semi-final between London Irish and Leicester at Sunbury and the player in question the Exiles skipper Gary Halpin.

With London Irish narrowly trailing the Tigers' 22-21 and the two packs poised to go down for a scrum, Halpin heard the PA announcer reading out the registration number of his Volvo, warning the owner of the car that it would be towed by the police if it was not immediately moved.

Halpin promptly disentangled himself from his team-mates and disappeared into the dressing room to locate his keys – eventually asking a friend in the crowd to do the honours for him and move the offending vehicle.

To add insult to injury, the Exiles lost the match 46-21.

ABOVE Gary Halpin wonders where he has left his car keys.

I haven't the foggiest...

Most players are more than ready for a hot bath and a pint by the end of a game, but for some 80 minutes doesn't seem to be nearly enough.

For example, take the strange case of Welsh full-back Bert Winfied, who managed to stay out on the pitch a full 10 minutes after the final whistle after Wales 1908 Home Nations encounter with England in Bristol.

BELOW Where's the ball mate? I'm sure Bert would sympathise with his footballing counterpart.

The game was badly affected by heavy fog but no-one realised how badly until the two teams had retired to the club house, only for the Welsh team to realise they were a man short.

A desperate search ensued and Winfied was finally found by his colleagues – still out on the pitch, peering into the dense fog.

Asked why the hell he was standing about while everyone else had widely gone indoors, the hapless full-back said he was convinced the game was still being played and the rest of his team-mates were attacking the English line.

Fruity frolics...

Players usually prefer to tear lumps out of the opposition but every now and then even the best of team-mates fall out. One notable incident came in 1997 when France faced Scotland in a Five Nations decider.

The Monday before the game French prop Christian Califano decided to play a little practical joke on giant second rower Olivier Merle – depositing a banana skin in the big man's boots when he wasn't looking.

Califano expected his ruse to be detected within minutes but heard nothing from the man mountain lock. The days passed and match day arrived and still nothing.

It transpired that Califano had dumped the banana skin in Merle's 'match day' boots – he had been wearing a different pair in training that week – and it was not until minutes before kick-off that the big lock finally discovered the rotting fruit remains.

Califano held his hand up immediately, Merle went ballistic and the pair had to be physically seperated by team-mates in the dressing room, who quite reasonably pointed out they had a rather important game to play and shouldn't they be focusing their energies on battering the Scots.

When Califano athletically sprinted out onto the Parc des Princes pitch, closely followed by Merle, people wrongly assumed they were both pumped up for the match.

ABOVE Christian Califano attempting another joke?

Pocket money...

Although Test matches are invariably fiercely-contested encounters with no shortage of blood, guts and thunder, some players still find the time for a little humour out on the pitch.

BELOW Australia v New Zealand, now where are those coins?

Perhaps two of the greatest exponents of this comedic approach to playing were Australia's Andy Slack and New Zealand's Stu Wilson who devised a cunning game to amuse themselves whenever the Wallabies and the All Blacks went head-to-head.

Both players would start the match with three Australian and New Zealand coins respectively in their pockets and would drop them at random from their pockets during the 80 minutes.

The winner of the game was the one who picked up the most of the other's coins — the loser, fittingly, having to put his hand in his pocket one last time to pay for the beers in the bar afterwards.

Spellbound...

With fifteen players on each side, communication is certainly the key to any successful team, as Wales realised in the 1970s when they thought they had devised an ingenious way of coordinating their back row moves.

With the legendary Gareth Edwards at scrum-half and Pontypool's Terry Cobner and Swansea's Trevor Evans as the two flankers, it was decided Edwards would call out any word beginning with P (for Pontypool) to signify a move on Edwards' side of the scrum and S (for Swansea) to let the forwards know they were moving on Evans' side.

ABOVE I'll have a 'P' please Bob. Gareth Edwards fools the opposition.

It was, it seemed, a flawless plan until one particular match. The referee blew for a scrum, the Welsh pack went down and rather unwisely, Edwards suddenly decided to shout 'psychology' – only to see both back row forwards haring off in completely opposite directions.

Short cut...

Making your senior debut is a tense and nerve-wracking moment for any young rugby player – which might explain the hilarious entrance made by Wales No.8 Scott Quinnell as a fresh-faced teenager back in the 1980s.

The story goes like this. Quinnell, just 18 at the time and still wet behind the ears, was named on the bench for his local club Llanelli and he was understandably keen to get out onto the pitch and make his mark.

BELOW Scott Quinnell runs with the ball.

But as the game wore on it seemed more and more unlikely he'd play any part in proceedings, until there was an injury to one of the forwards and an eager Quinnell was told to strip off and warm up.

After the once over from the physio, the injured player was carried off and Quinnell waved on, his young heart obviously bursting with pride.

Unfortunately for the future Wales and Lions star, something was seriously amiss. He looked down and saw his boots and socks were in order and then realised in horror he'd forgotten to put his shorts on.

Split personality...

Serious injuries are no laughing matter for the unfortunate player in question – but they are invariably a source of humour for team-mates and the opposition alike.

Take the example of scrum-half Chris Wright who was drafted in to play for Wasps in a London derby against Harlequins at late notice and must have wished by the end of the match that the call-up had never come.

In truth, Wright was having a shocker but just before half-time seemed to have redeemed himself with a sharp break that looked like leading to a try. But as he looked around for support, he was smashed to the ground by Quins' England flanker Peter Winterbottom.

Wright was dazed and confused after the hit and the Wasps physio duly informed skipper Dean Ryan: "It's no good, he doesn't know who he is."

Quick as a flash, Ryan responded: "Then tell him he's Gareth Edwards."

ABOVE Chris Wright or is that Gareth Edwards?

One in the eye...

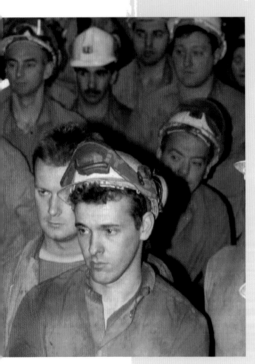

ABOVE Miners from Silverhill Colliery the year before the infamous clash with Daw Mill.

Another example of how one player's obvious misfortune can result in humour for everyone else came during the 1993 Coal Board Cup clash between Warwickshire's Daw Mill and Nottinghamshire's Silverhill Colliery.

During the second-half play had to be suddenly suspended when one of the Silverhill forwards went down clutching his face. The referee immediately went across to see what had happened, only to be told the player in question – Steve Bush – had lost his eye.

Bush, it transpired, had lost his left eye in a mining accident a few years previously and had now, under the weight of particularly heavy tackle, lost his glass eye somewhere on the pitch. A frantic search ensued but the glass eye remained lost and Bush decided to carry on with an empty eye socket.

Unfortunately for him, his brave decision was to go unrewarded as Daw Hill ran out 17-8 victors.

WEBB ELLIS

All black sees red...

New Zealand second row Cyril Brownlie has the dubious honour of being the first player ever to be sent off in an full international match.

The scene was Twickenham in 1925 and although no-one, including the players out on the pitch that day, was quite sure why the Kiwi received his marching orders against England, what is known is Brownlie ended up taking the first early bath in the game's history after some particularly 'robust' clashes between the two opposing packs in the early stages.

What is less well known is that there was another Brownlie on the pitch that day – Cyril's brother Maurice – who managed to last the full 80 minutes without any problems and went some way to redeeming the family honour with the third of the visitors' tries as the 14-man All Blacks defied the odds and ran out 17-11 winners.

BELOW The All Blacks 'Haka' in 1926.

A rum show...

Everyone knows rugby players only really hit top speed in the dash to the bar after the game itself has finished but some, it seems, cannot even wait that long for their favourite tipple.

One notable example was French forward Lucien Mias, who led the Tricolores on a tour of South Africa in 1958. Having unexpectedly drawn the first Test at Newlands when everyone predicted a handsome victory, the Springboks were widely tipped to exact retribution in the second and final Test but came unstuck and lost 9-5 against an inspired French team.

ABOVE England defeat a not so Lucien Mias-inspired France 1st March 1958.

Amazingly, Mias' preparations for the second-half of such a crucial game was to down half a bottle of rum in the dressing room. It didn't seem to affect the French skipper, though, with Mias to the fore for the next, all-important 40 minutes.

They said what?...

"You have fifteen players in a team. Seven hate your guts and the other eight are making their minds up." – Jack Rowell

"If they're going to call you this superhuman player or whatever and you believe it, then you should also believe it when they call you a tosser." – Martin Johnson

BELOW Serge Blanco.

"Far be it for me to criticise the referee but I saw him after the match and he was heading straight to the opticians. Guess who he bumped into on the way? Everyone." – Ian 'Mighty Mouse' McLauchlan

"I've never had major knee surgery on any other part of my body." – Gareth Edwards

"Losing to New South Wales is like masturbating, or losing a golf ball. You feel really remorseful afterwards but you know it will happen again if you're not careful." – Former Wallaby Chris 'Buddha' Handy

ABOVE "Playing in the second row doesn't require a lot of intelligence really." – Bill Beaumont

"Rugby is just like love. You have to give before you can take. And when you gave the ball it's like making love – you must think of the other's pleasure before your own." – Serge Blanco

"The Irish treat you like royalty before and after the game, and kick you to pieces during it." – Jeff Probyn

"For a New Zealand rugby man, I don't think there's any greater challenge than playing against the Springboks in South Africa." – John Mitchell

"There's no such thing as a lack of confidence. You either have it or you don't." – Rob Andrew

BELOW Lawrence Dallaglio.

"A good defender should be so mean that if he owned the Atlantic Ocean, he still wouldn't give you a wave." – Morne du Plessis

"It would be nice if, when we consistently win the ball, they learn to catch the pass." – Hooker Raphael Benitez laments his French back line

"I'm pleased to say I don't think about rugby all the time: just most of the time." – Lawrence Dallaglio

"(Will) Carling epitomises England's lack of skills. He has speed and bulk but plays like a castrated bull." – David Campese

"I'm just off for a quiet pint. Followed by 15 noisy ones." – Gareth Chilcott after his last game for Bath.

"Scotland is the Pacific nation of Britain." – Va'aiga Tuigamala

"I like to get in one really good tackle early in the game, even if it is late." – Ray Gravell

"Growing up in Wales meant two things to me: rugby on a Saturday and chapel on Sunday. The thought of doing anything else just never crossed our minds as youngsters." – Gareth Edwards

"The first half will be even. The second half will be even harder." – Terry Holmes

"If you're being poked in the eye or punched in the face, you act accordingly. Some back off, some go for the blood." – Scott Gibbs

ABOVE "Everything I have I owe to him and some day I'll get him back." – Victor Ubogu on Jack Rowell

They said what?...

BELOW Jason Leonard.

ABOVE "The convicts will smash the toffs."
— David Campese

"It's like having a Ferrari in the garage and going out and catching the bus."
— Tim Horan on the decision to leave the Millennium Stadium roof open during the 1999 World Cup.

"There he was, half his teeth missing, cheekbones smashed, hair all over the place, his skin looking as if it hadn't seen the sun for six months. He looked as if he'd just come out of a bunker."
— Laurent Cabannes pays tribute to Dean Richards

"We French score tries because we cannot kick penalties."
— Jean-Pierre Rives

"Of all the teams in the world you don't want to lose to, England's top of the list. If you beat them, it's because you cheat. If they beat you, it's because they've overcome your cheating." — Grant Fox

"I think Brian Moore's gnashers are the kind you get from a DIY shop and hammer in yourself." — Paul Rendall

"Look, I'm going back to union and you can't stop me."
— Scott Quinnell

"Being dropped and Take That splitting up on the same day is enough to finish anyone off."
— Martin Bayfield

"Dean Richards is nicknamed Warren, as in 'warren ugly bastard'." — Jason Leonard

"A sharp dresser who likes to show his biceps off in tight-fitting T-shirts that are a couple of sizes too small for him." — John Bentley on Neil Back

"Don't ask me about emotions in the Welsh dressing room. I'm someone who cries when he watches Little House on the Prairie." – Bob Norster

"The only thing you're ever likely to catch on the end of an English back line is chilblains." – David Campese

"I'm sure the lads will be glad to see him gone. There'll be more food for everyone else now!" – Austin Healey on Jason Leonard's retirement.

"It doesn't matter how quick you are, you cannot play rugby without a brain." – David Campese

"I played ten injury-free years between the ages of 12 and 22. Then it suddenly seemed like I was allergic to the 20th century." – Nigel Melville

"If you can't take a punch you should play table tennis." – Pierre Berbizier

"You need a mental toughness and probably don't need to be too bright." – Mark Regan on playing in the front row.

"My first responsibility is to myself. I want to satisfy myself by going out there and doing something you know no other player in the world has ever managed to pull off." – David Campese

ABOVE "The backs preen themselves and the forwards drink." – Dean Richards

WOULD YOU BELIEVE IT?
STRANGE STORIES FROM THE WORLDWIDE GAME

Chapter 2

Did you hear the one about the militant French team that decided to go on strike and then lost 350-0, or the fable of the butch All Black star who was knocked out by a flying bag of flour?

No? Then this chapter is essential reading as we delve into the more surreal side of rugby with some seriously strange stories and tall tales that wouldn't look out of place in an episode of the X-Files.

We've got countless improbable stories of exploding boots, pitch-invading dogs and Welsh passport scams that will amuse and bemuse in equal measure, not to mention the infamous case of the England player who failed to recognise a young Jonny Wilkinson.

So if you're looking for some of rugby's most bizarre moments, look no further.

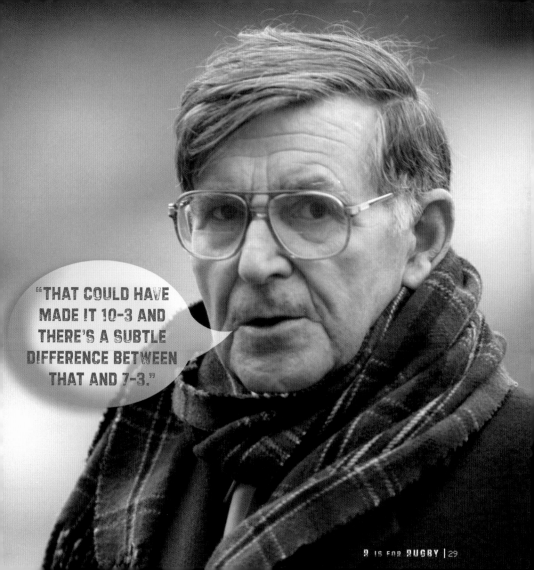

"THAT COULD HAVE MADE IT 10-3 AND THERE'S A SUBTLE DIFFERENCE BETWEEN THAT AND 7-3."

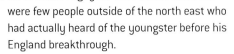

Jonny who?...

Jonny Wilkinson may be the one of the most famous rugby faces in the world these days, but it wasn't always the case for the injury-prone English World Cup-winner.

BELOW A fresh faced Jonny Wilkinson.

The Newcastle fly-half made his international debut in the Five Nations back in 1998 after playing just 58 minutes of senior rugby for the Falcons and there

were few people outside of the north east who had actually heard of the youngster before his England breakthrough.

Those in the dark definitely included veteran centre Jerry Guscott, who was more than a little bemused by Wilkinson's arrival for training on the Monday before the Scotland game at Murrayfield.

As the familiar faces in the England squad gathered round in readiness for a morning workout, Guscott noticed Wilkinson sheepishly making his entrance and immediately assumed the shy teenager was a schoolboy who had won a competition to meet his heroes in the England team.

Guscott was less than amused when he was informed the young man was actually one of the squad and, in the not-too-distant future, he'd be lining up alongside him in the England midfield.

The fame game...

Rugby can boast a host of famous fans – but it can also lay claim to more than its fair share of famous players.

Former American president Bill Clinton played in the second row while he was a Rhodes Scholar at Oxford University and also represented his home town club Little Rock RFC in Arkansas, while the late Pope John Paul II won a full cap for his native Poland as a youngster.

Less proudly, however, rugby can also claim ex-Ugandan leader Idi Amin among its playing ranks – the infamous dictator sat on the bench for the East African team that faced the 1955 British Lions.

The first Olympics to feature rugby were the London Games of 1908 – although it was hardly what anyone could call a testing tournament. Only two teams – England and Australia – actually bothered to enter, with the Wallabies beating the host nation in the 'final'.

ABOVE Ex-President Bill Clinton.

Irish spiked...

Despite boasting a physique that no-one could ever call robust, famous comedian Spike Milligan was a devoted player in his younger days and turned out for the London Irish 'B' team before the outbreak of the Second World War.

After he hung up his boots, Milligan and actor Richard Harris could often be spotted at Sunbury cheering on the Exiles.

American football began life as rugby and perhaps would not be in existence today if had not been for President Theodore Roosevelt, who threatened to ban the game in 1905 after seeing pictures of a violent clash between Sarthmore and Pennsylvania.

That sparked the gradual evolution of rugby into gridiron – including allowing forward passes – and the emergence of padding, timeouts and cheerleaders.

ABOVE The late great Spike Milligan.

Thirty five's a crowd...

One of the smallest crowds on record for an international rugby match must surely be the 35 supporters, who were said to have turned up to watch the Springboks take on the American Eagles in New York in 1981.

The South Africans had already played two games in the States but eager to sidestep the ever-present anti-apartheid protests, it was decided to switch the third and final game from its scheduled Saturday kick-off to Friday.

The venue was also changed in a bid to fool the protesters but proved such a successful ploy that only 35 fans knew the game was even on. The record books show the Springboks emerged 38-7 winners.

The dead ball line was introduced to the sport in 1891 after farcical scenes during a game between Bristol and Newport.

According to folklore, a Bristol player ran a full 300 metres beyond the try line – prompting the authorities to quickly prescribe a second line to avoid future confusion.

ABOVE The Springboks celebrate a much larger crowd!

The politics game...

When South Africa toured England in 1906 there was uproar after the Test match between the two countries.

The game ended in a draw but was played in such terrible conditions, there were furious calls to the Under Secretary of State for the fixture to be replayed. And his name? A certain Winston Churchill.

BELOW Argentina take on the South Africans.

Argentina are nicknamed the Pumas because of the big cat motif on their shirts, but the truth is they should be known as the Jaguars. On their 1965 tour of South Africa, a journalist noticed the cat design but wrongly assumed it was a puma, rather than a jaguar, and coined the nickname in one of this reports. The name, however, stuck.

Points bonanza...

Pundits often refer to teams having run up 'a cricket score' when one side inflicts a particularly heavy defeat on their opponents, but even some cricket teams would have struggled to emulate the scorelines conceded by French third division side Vergt in 1984.

With the club protesting at the suspension of four of their leading players and operating the rugby equivalent of a 'go slow', Vergt were beaten 236-0 by Gujah-Misters in a league clash. Seven days later, however, they outdid themselves, going down 350-0 to Lavardac, breaking every known rugby record in the process.

Scotland prop David Sole failed to turn up for a disciplinary hearing in 1995 much to the annoyance of the SRU. His excuse? He had to stay at home and baby-sit.

BELOW Sadly for England David Sole turned up for Scotland's Grand Slam deciding clash with England in 1990.

Wooly jumpers?...

Innovation and invention are the watch words of any successful rugby coach and could certainly be applied to Daryl Haberecht, an Australian who cause a storm in the game in the 1970s with one of the most bizarre tactics the sport has ever seen.

Haberecht was the coach of New South Wales Country and unveiled his unusual move in a 1975 game against arch-rivals Sydney.

Trailing 20-16, Country were awarded a tap penalty 40 metres from the Sydney line and to the bemusement of their opposition, a dozen Country players lined up together, turned their backs on Sydney and took the tap. At this point, the Country players then began haring off in different directions.

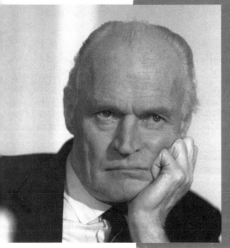

BELOW Sir Ewart Bell of the International Rugby Board Committee looking decidedly unimpressed by the 'ball up the jumper' routine.

What no-one knew was the fact one of them — number eight Greg Cornelsen — had tucked the ball up his jumper. He was eventually tackled but the ruse led directly to the match-winning try.

A number of Australian sides copied the move in the following weeks until the International Board put its foot down, decided it was against the spirit of the game and banned the unusual if successful tactic.

Flour power...

The Springboks 1981 tour of New Zealand was plagued by anti-apartheid protests, but it was an unfortunate All Black who was to suffer most from the depth of public feeling at the South African's visit.

During the third Test, a light aircraft began flying over the Eden Park stadium, bombarding the players and fans alike with flour bombs. One of these projectiles hit Kiwi Gary Knight, briefly knocking him out.

Rugby players volunteered in their thousands for both of the World Wars, so it should perhaps be no surprise that Edgar Mobbs, who played for Northampton, signalled to his men that it was time to go over the top in the first great conflict by kicking a rugby ball into no man's land.

Half-time toast...

ABOVE Sign on a Cape Town beach from the 1980s depicting a white-only area..

They do things differently in France – as the players of Racing Club de France proved in 1990 as the club contested the final of the French Club Championship.

Despite having failed to win the trophy for 31 years, the Racing team were so confident of victory against Agen at half-time that they decided to celebrate with champagne out on the pitch. Fortunately for the cocky Racing players, they won the match – but only after Agen had taken them into extra-time.

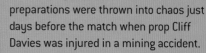

Papers please...

BELOW Will the real Cliff Davies please stand up? Cliff from the 1950s.

In these days of frequent international travel, most people have passports but it wasn't always the case — even if you were an international rugby player.

Back in 1946, Wales were scheduled to play France in Paris but their preparations were thrown into chaos just days before the match when prop Cliff Davies was injured in a mining accident.

It was quickly decided to call-up Davies cousin Billy Jones. The only problem was Jones didn't have a passport and there was no time to go through the official channels and secure him one.

However, the cousins bore a striking family resemblance and it was agreed Jones would travel to France under with Davies' papers.

The ruse worked perfectly. So perfectly, in fact, that all the subsequent match reports of the game referred to Jones and Davies. The French authorities were clearly none the wiser.

Barking mad...

When you're facing the All Blacks in their own back yard you need all the help you can get – which is exactly what the British Lions got in 1971 in the unusual shape of a dog.

With the series all square at 1-1 going into the the third and potentially decisive Test, the Lions battled their way into a 13-3 lead.

ABOVE The Lions on tour 1971.

Predictably the New Zealanders threw the kitchen sink at the visitors in the second-half and looked certain to score through centre Howard Joseph, until the dog (an unidentified boxer) ran out onto the pitch and attempted to bite the Kiwi player.

Joseph leapt over the dog, fell to the ground and the Lions cover managed to get back and snuff out the danger. The dog disappeared – as had the All Blacks chances of rescuing the match. The Lions held on to win 13-3, drew the fourth Test the following week and, thanks in small part to a certain canine, became the first Lions side to win a series against the mighty All Blacks.

Post traumatic stress...

The woodwork of the posts has broken the hearts of countless of unfortunate goalkickers, but it was a real match-saver for England when they entertained France at Twickenham in 1993.

ABOVE Jonathan Webb, keeping a safe hand on the ball.

Playing poorly in front of their own fans, England had already conceded two first-half tries at HQ when the woodwork made its first dramatic intervention on proceedings.

With the referee ready to blow for half-time, England were awarded a penalty and full-back Jonathan Webb stepped forward for the three-pointer.

His kick, however, hit the crossbar and bounced back, landing fortuitously into the arms of winger Ian Hunter, who scampered over for an outrageously lucky try.

But the woodwork's work was not yet done. England held a slight 16-15 lead after the break but were still performing badly and it seemed the French might break through at any moment.

The home defence was creaking but with time running out, France opted for the drop kick route, first the prolific Didier Cambarabero and then Aubin Heuber unleashing well-struck efforts only to see them come back off the posts. And in contrast to England in the first-half, there was on-one on hand to pounce on the rebounds and France went down 16-15.

The exploding boot...

Rugby is a game full of big hits and bone-crunching knocks and it is usually the players rather than their equipment that come off the worse for wear.

One hilarious exception to this rule came on the All Blacks' 1960 tour of South Africa and the story goes like this.

The New Zealanders arrived for one of their midweek games only for their legendary kicker and full-back Don Clarke to discover in the dressing room that he'd left his boots behind at the team hotel.

There was a brief panic as Clarke was the lynch pin of the team but everyone breathed a sight of relief when one of his colleagues offered to lend him his spare pair of boots.

The problem was the spare pair were not exactly in tip top condition – they were basically falling apart – but Clarke had little choice since he had no time to get back to the hotel and took to the field in the hand-me-downs.

Minutes into the match and the All Blacks were awarded a penalty. Clarke stepped forward and, as was his style, gave the ball an almighty thump.

Team-mates recalled hearing what they thought was a small explosion but when the looked up they realised the borrowed boot had disintegrated on impact into numerous shreds of leather, now scattered all over the pitch.

ABOVE Jonah Lomu shows off his boots.

Soviet sanction...

BELOW Oleg
Shukaikailov of Russia
probably wished the
sanctions had lasted a
touch longer.

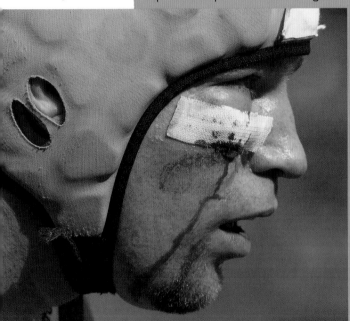

When famous Welsh outfit Llanelli sent a team to the USSR for the 1957 World Youth Games in Moscow, the players could have had no idea the impact their trip would have on the game in the communist state. Reports say that Llanelli's bad-tempered and occasionally violent clash with Romanian side Grivita Rosie so appalled communist officials that they decided to ban the game in the USSR for nearly 30 years.

Rugby has attracted the great and the good over the years but few more instantly recognisable and respected than Nelson Mandela, who was one of the record 105,000-strong crowd that packed into Ellis Park to witness the first Test between South Africa and the Lions in 1955.

Too much too young...

Just like policeman, rugby players seem to be getting younger and younger these days but even the modern generation of fresh-faced upstarts would struggle to hold a candle to Scotland's Kenneth MacLeod.

A dynamic and exciting centre, MacLeod was a tender 15-years-old back in 1903 and still studying at Fettes College when Scotland called him up for a match with the Welsh. He didn't play in the match, however, because his headmaster refused him permission on the reasonable grounds he was far too young.

Unperturbed, the Scottish selectors tried to pick MacLeod once again two years later – ironically to face Wales – but once again his dutiful headmaster put a spanner in the works and the youngster was denied his first taste of international rugby for a second time.

MacLeod finally did make his debut in late 1905 while he was a student at Cambridge

ABOVE An early portrayal of the Scotland team taking on England c1900.

(and finally away from his protective headmaster's clutches) and played against the touring All Blacks just three months short of his 18th birthday. For the record, he went on to win 10 caps for Scotland before retiring at the grand old age of 20.

David and Goliath...

BELOW Steaua
Bucharest rugby team
celebrate winning the
Romanian rugby
championship in June
2003, three years after
the hapless Dorchester
Gladiators arrived.

There have been few bigger mismatches in rugby history than the strange case of the 2000 clash between the unheralded Dorchester Gladiators and one of Romania's leading sides.

On tour in Romania over Easter, the Gladiators were offered a friendly game by a local embassy official they meet, which the team gratefully accepted.

Unfortunately for the modest tourists, the game was to be staged at the National Stadium on live TV against Steaua Bucharest, the best team in the country.

It quickly dawned on the Gladiators that there had been an enormous (and potentially very embarrassing) misunderstanding and they were clearly way out of their depth.

But despite their protests that the match would make David and Goliath look like a fair fight, the game went ahead and even though Steaua did the decent thing and eased up in the second-half, the hapless Gladiators were still thumped 60-17.

Bug bears...

Clive Woodward's attention to detail and preparation are legendary but what many people don't realise is the former England coach could be also be described as a little on the paranoid side.

During England's ultimately successful World Cup campaign Down Under in 2003, Woodward was so worried about rugby's equivalent of industrial espionage that he insisted that the team's meeting rooms be swept for electronic listening devices before he would start to discuss tactics.

The Australian newspapers had a field day when they got wind of Woodward's worry but the man himself was unrepentant.

"Sometimes people don't understand the huge stakes we're playing for," he said. "We don't want to take any chances – and we don't. It's just common sense. We've done it for a couple of years now and it's our standard way of operating. It's just security and we take security very seriously."

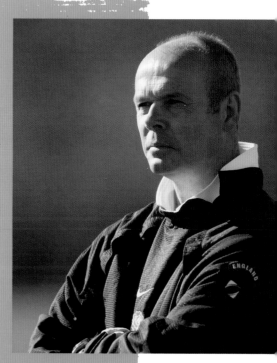

ABOVE Clive Woodward ponders his World Cup winning tactics.

They said what?...

"Props are as crafty as a bag of weasels.
— Bill McLaren

"Prop forwards don't get Valentine's cards for religious reasons — God made them ugly!"
— Anonymous

"New Zealand rugby is a colorful game since you get all black.. and blue." — Anonymous

"Rugby is a physical game. Sometimes a bit of handbagging can clear the air." — Alex Wyllie

"Have a go, you mug. That means, don't die wondering whether you were good enough to win. Don't wait until you've lost to see if you can win."
— Bob Dwyer

"If you didn't know him, you wouldn't know who he was." — Nigel Starmer-Smith

"Rugby is like an organised orgy."
— Anonymous

"The amateur rugby union player has an inalienable right to play like a pillock." — Dick Greenwood

ABOVE "South Africa were a disgrace. Corne Krige as captain targeted the entire England team. It was all rather Jurassic."
— Stuart Barnes

"A game for ruffians played by gentlemen." — Anonymous

"Dusty Hare kicked 19 of the 17 points."
— David Coleman

"When a referee is in doubt, he is justified in deciding against the side which makes most noise. They are probably in the wrong."
– Anonymous

"I will handle things the Brian Clough way. Whenever a player has a problem we will talk about it for 20 minutes and I will listen carefully to what he has to say. Then we'll agree that I was right."
– Sir Clive Woodward

"That could have made it 10-3 and there's a subtle difference between that and 7-3." – Bill McLaren

"I don't like this new law because your first instinct when you see a man on the ground is to go down on him." – Murray Mexted

"I prefer rugby to soccer. I enjoy the violence in rugby, except when they start biting each other's ears off."
– Elizabeth Taylor

"It shows what a hot seat that number nine jersey has been."
– Nigel Starmer-Smith

"The relationship between the Welsh and the English is based on trust and understanding. They don't trust us and we don't understand them." – Dudley Wood

"The quickest way to take the edge off your game is to train." – Willie Duggan

"To play rugby league you need three things: a good pass, a good tackle and a good excuse." – Anonymous

ABOVE "A player of ours has been proven guilty of biting. That's a scar that will never heal."
– Andy Robinson

They said what?...

BELOW Bill McLaren.

"Rugby is a game for big buggers; if you're not a big bugger, you get hurt. I wasn't a big bugger but I was a fast bugger and therefore I avoided the big buggers."
— Spike Milligan

"Playing rugby at school I once fell on a loose ball and, through ignorance and fear, held on despite a fierce pummelling. After that it took me months to convince my team-mates I was a coward."
— Peter Cook

"Rugby is a good occasion for keeping thirty bullies far from the centre of the city." — Oscar Wilde

"Rugby is a physical manifestation of our rules of life comradeship, honest endeavour, and a staunch, often ponderous allegiance to fair play." — Colin Welland

"Serious sport has nothing do with fair play. It is war minus the shooting."
— George Orwell

"He's like a mad ferret." — Bill McLaren

"Rugby is a wonderful show: dance, opera and, suddenly, the blood of a killing." — Richard Burton

ABOVE "(Wales did not even have) enough imagination to thump someone in the line-up when the referee wasn't looking."
— JPR Williams

"In rugby each side is allowed to put in a certain amount of assault and battery and do things to its fellow man which, if done elsewhere, would result in 14 days without the option." — PG Woodhouse

JAMES IN THE DUNGEON

WHEN WAS THE LAST TIME YOU PLAYED

Chapter 3

THE REFEREES
A TRIBUTE TO WHISTLE BLOWERS WORLDWIDE

You've got to feel sorry for rugby referees. No, really. They spend 80 minutes being harangued by both sets of players who suddenly find common ground in their mutual mistrust of the man with the shiny and overactive whistle, only to face the wrath of disgruntled and invariably furious fans once the match is finally over.

By anyone's standards it's a thankless task and, from time to time, a dangerous one too. Rugby players after all are not renowned for their pacifist tendencies.

Why referees across the world subject themselves to the abuse, put downs and confrontations remains a mystery. Perhaps it's a perverse sense of masochism or maybe they're simply trying to avoid going shopping with the wife on Saturday afternoon.

But whatever their reasons, rugby needs referees and their invaluable if occasionally controversial contribution to the game worldwide.

In this chapter, you'll read about the over zealous official who sent his own linesman off, the whistle blower who felt the force of a Springbok fan's displeasure and the man who, believe it or not, proved once and for all that some referee's actually have a sense of humour.

Knowing the rules?...

'Do you even know the rules, ref?' is a common refrain from disgruntled fans worldwide and in the case of English whistle-blower Ken Pattison at Murrayfield in 1976 the answer was unfortunately a resounding no.

Pattison's very public faux pas came as Scotland took on the French. The match was played in near gale force conditions which made kicking a complete lottery.

With Scotland 3-0 up however, they were awarded a penalty by Pattison and despite the wind and the distance, Andy Irvine decided he'd have a pop at goal. Now remember this was in the days before kicking tees, so

BELOW Andy Irvine goes in for a tackle.

Irvine asked his prop Ian McLauchlan to hold the ball for the kick, which defied the elements and sailed over.

The Scottish fans went wild until they realised Pattison had disallowed the goal because he said McLauchlan had been lying in front of the ball and was therefore offside. If he'd been more familiar with the rules he would have known McLauchlan's position was perfectly legal.

France went on to win the game 13-6 and Pattison was never asked to take charge of an international match again.

No-one is safe...

Even the most card-happy official, keen to ensure a steady flow of players for an early bath would be hard pressed to outdo the referee of a 1967 game, in which he sent his own linesman off for misconduct.

The match in question was a clash between Royal Naval Engineering College and Camborne and the poor, unfortunate linesman was a man called George Riches, who was himself a former member of the England international panel and a familiar face on the circuit in the south west.

For this game, Riches was running the Camborne line when, in the second-half, a couple of opposing forwards started having a dust-up. Eager to nip the problem in the bid, Riches went over and tried to restrain one of the offenders before things go out of hand.

Unfortunately for him, by the time the match referee arrived on the scene, the melee looked much worse than it really was and Riches was promptly sent off for fighting even though in fact he was the innocent party.

"The referee did send him off," said a Camborne official after the match. "But from what I saw of the incident, this was not necessary. George was only trying to keep the peace." Riches kept his views on the incident to himself.

ABOVE Simon Shaw (left) the England lock is sent to an early bath by Nigel Williams.

He's behind you...

Referees have a hard job at the best of times and it's a rare occasion indeed when the man in the middle doesn't infuriate at least one set of supporters during a game.

For their part, fans tend to limit their annoyance with the whistle bowlers to dark grumblings and, perhaps, some colourful hand signals. Sadly this was not the case in 2002 when South Africa took on New Zealand in Durban.

BELOW David McHugh checking to see if the coast is clear.

The referee that day was David McHugh and after awarding the All Blacks a hotly-contested penalty try and then denying the home side what looked like a legitimate try of their own, he was not what you'd call flavour of the month with the Springbok faithful.

Cue the shameful intervention of 40-something South African 'fan' Pieter van Zyl who slipped past the stewards and invaded the pitch, attacking McHugh from behind and dislocating his shoulder.

Zyl was quickly wrestled to the ground by Springbok and All Black players alike and arrested but the damage had already been done. He did, at least, receive a lifetime ban from all South African rugby games.

Odds and sods...

Whistle-happy referees are the scourge of players around the world but officials weren't actually equipped with whistles for the first 50 years of the game until some bright spark suggested the new piece of kit. Wags have suggested they've been making up for lost time ever since.

'Waste not, want not' is an old saying and one obviously taken to heart by Welsh referee Derek Bevan when he took charge of the 1995 World Cup clash between South Africa and Australia. When Bevan signalled the start of the game, he blew a whistle that had been used by another Welsh referee – Albert Freethy – 70 years earlier during an international between England and New Zealand.

ABOVE Derek Bevan issuing orders.

Time please...

Referees are not always the callous and unsympathetic animals they are portrayed as. For instance, what about the man who took pity on the Corby Rugby Club in 1989? Touring the north of England, Corby were playing Whitby but with a mere seven minutes of the second-half gone they were already 80 points to nil down. Step forward the referee, who abandoned the match after ruling the Corby players were too drunk to continue.

A hill to climb...

If you thought controversy about refereeing decisions was a modern phenomenon, you would be very wrong indeed. Even back in the late 1800s, with the game still in its infancy, the men with the whistles were causing outrage and uproar.

One such contentious match occurred in 1889 when England entertained the touring New Zealand Natives side at Blackheath. The referee on the day was Rowland Hill, who also happened to be the RFU secretary, and as the Kiwis learnt to their cost, he was not the kind of man to be argued with.

BELOW The famous scoreboard at Blackheath.

Hill first enraged the tourists by awarding two tries to the home side when, on both occasions, it was clear to everyone that a New Zealand, rather than English hand had touched the ball down. To add insult to injury, Hill then awarded a third English try after played had been stopped while a new pair of shorts were found for one of the home team.

At this point three of the New Zealanders walked off in disgust and jobsworth Hill demanded a written apology for their actions. The poor Kiwis were condemned in the press for their unsportsmanlike protest and the tour ended in acrimony and recrimination.

Dropped right in it...

For a referee to award one drop goal that wasn't could be described as careless but to do it twice in the same match is almost unforgivable, as hapless official Mike Titcomb discovered when he presided over the Ireland versus Wales clash in Dublin in 1968.

Titcomb's first clanger came midway through the first-half when Irish fly-half Mike Gibson attempted a drop which, in Titcomb's defence, did go through the posts. The problem was it also hit a Welsh hand on the way which, according to the rules of the game, means no score.

The Ireland fans obviously did not object, however, and the game carried on.

That is it continued without incident until the second-half, when legendary Wales scrum-half Gareth Edwards thought he'd copy Gibson and have a drop at goal himself. This time there were no touches on the ball en route but it didn't matter because it was obvious to everyone in the ground that Edwards' effort had sailed wide.

Obvious to everyone except Titcomb, who blew his whistle to signal the points. Lansdowne Road was in uproar, missiles were hurled down onto the pitch and fans broke through the touch-line cordons to protest.

In the end, Ireland held on for a 9-6 victory but Titcomb still had to be escorted from the pitch by a ring of policemen.

ABOVE Mike Gibson pictured in 1966.

Three in one?...

It is still a notable occasion when the referee does not make it through the full 80 minutes of a game and has to be replaced. It is almost unheard of for three different men to be in charge of the whistle during a single match.

The record books of New Zealand rugby, however, do mention one such game.

It was the Bush versus Wanganui fixture of 1957 and a certain Roy Rice was named as the original match referee. All was going well until Rice collided with a player in the process of scoring a try and had to leave the field for treatment.

Into the breach stepped Leith Parker, who was running the line and also happened to be the Bush president. It soon became apparent that Rice would not be able to resume his duties and with Parker far from what anyone could neutral, a desperate search for another official began.

Eventually a sufficiently qualified man by the name of Wray Hewitt was located and he became the third match referee on a very bizarre afternoon of rugby.

BELOW Probably more of a common occurrence in football rather than rugby as this chap will attest.

I'm off!...

Thankfully red cards remain a rarity in rugby. What is rarer still is when a player decides to send himself off, as former Ireland international and Lions prop Gerry McLoughlin did in a cup match back in 1988.

By now McLoughlin, also known as 'Ginger', was retired from the first-class game but playing on for Wales club side Gilfach Goch and the team had a big Challenge Cup game at Laugharne.

Not long into the game there was a bit of a dust-up between the two sets of forwards which required the intervention of the referee, Roy Rees. Lecturing the numerous culprits about the need for a good, clean game, Rees said: "Push off and let's get on with the match." Unfortunately McLoughlin took this to mean he was destined for an early bath and he quietly trudged off in shame.

It was only when the two packs prepared for a scrum some minutes after Ginger's self-imposed exit that everyone, including Rees, realised what had happened. Luckily for the premature McLoughlin, the 14 men of Gilfach still emerged victorious.

ABOVE At least a dejected Mat Keenan of Western Samoa had actually been sent off.

Man in the middle...

Contrary to popular opinion, not all rugby referees are as stupid as they look and from time to time the men in the middle can actually show signs of intelligence way beyond the grasp of your average front row player.

One such moment came during France's 1999 tour of Argentina for a sevens tournament. Now Argentinean fans are what you could politely call passionate. So passionate in fact they had to be kept off the pitch for one of the French games by a moat and a huge fence and the atmosphere inside the ground was decidedly volatile.

The referee for the game was respected international official Chris White but even he could little about the barrage of fruit that was continually thrown by the crowd onto the pitch.

France, perhaps unwisely, contrived to score a last-minute try in the corner and as the French kicker prepared to take the conversion right next to the fence and moat, he was predictably pelted with fruit. The Frenchman turned plaintively to White and asked what he was going to do about it. White – who had already been hit with an orange – replied: "I'm going to stand in the middle of the pitch while you take the conversion."

BELOW Very spirited Argentinian fans.

Ball games...

A sense of humour is an absolute must for any referee who wants to cope with the highs and lows of trying to control a game of rugby. It also comes in very handy when you are trying to avoid answering awkward questions about that grey area that is the interpretation of the laws.

ABOVE England practice their scrum hoping to evade any new laws.

At the start of the 1997 season, the three Tri-Nations heavyweights of New Zealand, Australia and South Africa decided to introduce a new law that, quite reasonably, outlawed the grabbing of a player's testicles.

The problem according to the sceptical press, however, was how exactly would the poor referees be able to see someone committing such an offence, especially if it occurred at the bottom of a ruck with bodies lying all over the place.

A leading southern hemisphere referee was found to placate the news men, presented to the assembled hacks and asked him whether, in his opinion, the new law was workable. "It is hard to detect," he admitted. "It depends on how much water is coming out of a player's eyes."

Lion tamer...

The British Lions that faced the Springboks in 1974 were arguably the greatest of any of the Home Union touring teams to leave these shores. They didn't lose a single game on the tour but they were deprived of a 100 per cent record thanks to the intervention of a South African referee by the name of Max Baise.

The Lions went into the fourth and final Test of the series in Johannesburg already 3-0 up but were desperate to complete a whitewash. The Springboks were equally desperate to save some face and with the game tied 13-13 in the dying minutes, it seemed the honours would be shared.

That is until celebrated Irish flanker Fergus Slattery made a break and scored what the Lions thought was the winning try. But as they looked around they realised Baise had ruled out the score, claiming he'd already blown for full-time before Slattery had crossed the line. The Lions had been denied and their tour record would forever read played 22, won 21, drawn one. "The decision showed the ref had some brains in his head," joked one Springbok fan after the game. "He has to stay in this country after the Lions have gone home."

BELOW The British Lions squad – 1974.

Going, going, gone...

Referees can have as short a fuse as some of the players they are charged to control – judging by actions of whistle-blower George Crawford.

The scene was a 1985 Anglo-Welsh clash between Bristol and Newport and it was an ill-tempered game which culminated in a mass brawl. But rather than deal with the melee, Crawford simply walked off the pitch and refused to come back once order had been restored.

The game, however, did go ahead when a local referee in the crowd volunteered to do the honours.

Neutral referees for international matches made their first appearance way back in 1881 but it was to be a further eight years before they were joined neutral touch judges.

Two minute wonder...

Most players who get themselves sent off by the referee believe they are hard done by, but Saracens Kieran Roche probably had a point when he was sent to the dressing room during a game against Bath.

Roche only came onto the pitch from the bench in the 76th minute of the match but less than two minutes later got his marching orders from the referee. His crime? Persistent infringement.

ABOVE One of the first of a noble breed: Rugby Union referee and administrator G Rowland Hill from 1890.

French farce...

Refereeing can be a dangerous business if the players prove to be unhappy with some of the decisions you've made but it is not just during the 80 minutes of the match itself that the officials need to be mindful.

Take the 1991 World Cup quarter-final clash between France and England in Paris, refereed by New Zealander David Bishop. A tense, occasionally violent clash which England won 19-10, most neutrals agreed Bishop had done well in what were demanding circumstances.

Not so French coach Daniel Dubroca, who was fuming at his side's disappointing capitulation and quite literally collared the Kiwi official outside the dressing rooms after the game. Allegations of an assault followed and although Bishop refused to comment on the incident, it was obvious the New Zealander had, at the very least, been unceremoniously pounced on.

"I was simply congratulating the referee," Dubroca insisted later. "If I touched him, it was a fraternal gesture." Despite his protests of innocence, Dubroca resigned soon after the incident.

ABOVE Daniel Dubroca in his playing days.

Replay milestone...

The advent of video technology has, for the bigger fixtures at least, meant the team of officials at a game has expanded from three to four with the arrival of the video referee.

The first ever international game to feature the video ref was in New Zealand in June 2000 when the All Blacks took on Tonga.

The match referee was England's Steve Lander and his replay pal in the stands Kiwi Steve Walsh, who was called into action for the first time to rule whether All Black skipper Todd Blackadder had grounded the ball for a try after a pile-up of bodies. Walsh awarded the score and history was made.

Norman Sanson earned himself a place in the refereeing record books when he became the first official to send off two players in the same international fixture.

The game was the 1977 Wales versus Ireland Championship clash and the players banished from the pitch Wales' Geoff Wheel and Ireland's Willie Duggan. The miscreant pair were dismissed for fighting.

ABOVE Referee Steve Lander.

Mr T...

Hard-drinking Denis Thatcher will be best remembered as the husband of the Iron Lady but what few people realise is he was an experienced rugby referee before his wife found political fame.

In fact, Sir Denis ran the line in 1956 for an Anglo-French clash in the Stade Colombes in Paris before he hung up his flag and whistle and moved into Number Ten.

BELOW Jonathan Davies in action for Cardiff.

One of the best one-liners ever from a referee has to be the joke made by an official who was given charge of a match at Gordonstoun School in 1995.

At the time the Gordonstoun skipper was no other than rugby-playing royal Peter Phillips (Princess Anne's son), whose duty is was to toss up at the start of the game with the opposing captain. Turning to the blue-blooded youngster with his coin in hand, the referee enquired: "Grandmother or tails, sir?"

Referees are't paranoid...

Referees aren't paranoid – everybody really does hate them. Which is hardly surprising when some of the game's most respected pundits and writers seem so determined to undermine them.

Take Wales legend Jonathan Davies, who once famously joked on 'A Question of Sport': "I think you enjoy the game more if you don't know the rules. Anyway, you're on the same wavelength as the referee."

Davies, however, is only the latest in a long line of ref bashers. For example, Michael Green wrote in 1960 in 'The Art of Coarse Rugby': "The first half is invariably much longer than the second. This is partly because of the late kick-off but is also caused by the unfitness of the referee." With friends like these, who needs enemies?

IN THE HOSPITAL

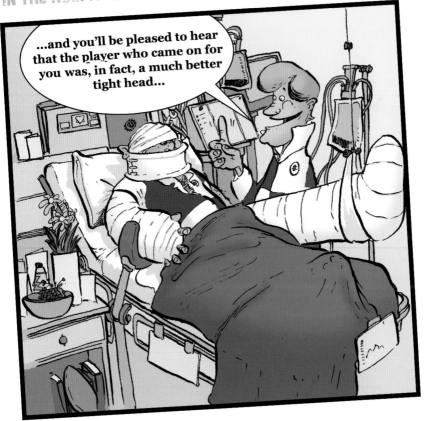

WHEN THE FINAL WHISTLE BLOWS

If you thought rugby games were brutal, disorganised and chaotic events with little or no semblance of order or decency, you should see the players in the bar after the match.

Yes, there's absolutely no doubt about it, rugby is as wild, wonderful and wacky away from the pitch as it is on it. Just ask the England forward who ended up in a French hospital after being duped by his team-mates at a post-match dinner or the former Scotland skipper who discovered he was not quite the cunning linguist he thought.

This chapter celebrates the most outrageous, comical and plain disastrous tales the game has throw up over the years as we delve into the strange cases of Clive Woodward's insomnia Down Under, the unfortunate Italian thief who had a very bad day at the office and the Irish club team who toured Russia and made a killing.

So if you're one of those people who believe a match is 80 minutes of lost drinking time, read on. A trawl through rugby's archives

Set up...

Most people would agree – rugby is not a game for the feint-hearted or those of a nervous disposition. But even some of the most fearsome players on the pitch, such as Wales hooker Bobby Windsor, prove to be not quite as fearless once the final whistle goes.

BELOW Bobby Windsor passing the ball – or is that the mascot, to Gareth Edwards.

Windsor, also known as 'The Duke', was selected for the 1974 British Lions tour to South Africa and during the tour travelled with the rest of the squad for a safari of the world-famous Kruger National Park. A man from the Valleys more used to foxes and badgers, Windsor made no secret of the fact he was more than a little apprehensive at the prospect of coming face-to-face with one of the park's resident predators.

One night, when everyone had gone to bed, Windsor was woken by a huge roar. This was quickly followed by the twinkling of broken glass and 'The Duke' suddenly felt something pawing at his leg. Blinded by fear, he lashed out at the uninvited furry intruder, desperately punching and kicking in the dark until he collapsed, exhausted to the floor.

When the lights came on there was a mixture of astonishment and hilarity as Windsor and his room-mates realised he had just dismembered one of the Lions' toy mascots. Outside, there was only amusement from the three players who had set 'The Duke' up – throwing the mascot in after smashing the window with a log they'd found lying around.

A close shave...

Rugby players are renowned for their fondness for a pint or twelve after a game and England prop Colin Smart must have wished he'd stuck to the beer after a Five Nations clash against France in the early 1980s.

At dinner following the match in Paris, the England team were each presented with a bottle of aftershave by their French hosts to commemorate the game. While Smart was otherwise occupied, his wily team-mates quickly emptied their bottles, quietly refilled them with water and then challenged Smart to follow their lead and down his bottle. Eager not to lose face, the burly Cornish prop accepted the challenge and duly drained the original contents of his bottle.

ABOVE Colin Smart looking forward to a few beers.

Naturally, the rest of the England team fell about in stitches as Smart began to look much the worse for wear but the smiles were soon wiped off their faces when he had to be rushed to hospital to have his stomach pumped by anxious French doctors.

Fortunately the hapless forward was quickly restored to rude health – although his reputation never fully recovered.

Parlez vous francais?...

BELOW Gavin Hastings clears his lines – rugby lines that is.

Gavin Hastings enjoyed a long and distinguished career with Scotland and the Lions but his reputation did not make him immune to the practical jokes of his mischievous team-mates.

In 1995 Hastings took his side to face the French at the Parc des Princes and thanks in no small part to his own long-range try, the Scots recorded their first win in Paris for 30 years.

To their credit, the French were very gracious in defeat and eager to repay the compliment, Hastings wanted to give his post-match speech at dinner in French. Unfortunately he didn't speak a word of the language, so he press ganged second row Damian Cronin, who had been played in France for a couple of seasons, into action as his translator.

When the time came, Hastings stood up and thanked his hosts for their warm welcome. Cronin translated and the crowd went wild with a mixture of cheering and laughter.

Pleased but perplexed at the reaction, Hastings sat down none the wiser. It was only later in the evening that he learnt what Cronin had really said to the hosts, which went along the lines of 'Once I have finished this speech, I shall be taking my wife upstairs and making mad, passionate love to her'.

Sea sickness...

Before Clive Woodward was leading England to
World Cup glory, he was a fine player in his own right and played for England and
the Lions before he took up coaching.

During his playing career, Woodward had a spell in Australia with the famous
Manly club and although Englishmen playing Down Under were certainly a rarity
in those days, the club were keen to help him settle in the area so he could
concentrate on his rugby.

BELOW Clive preparing
himself for a restful
nights sleep!

As part of that, Woodward was installed
in a beautiful beach-front flat close to
the Manly Surf Club with stunning views
of the coastline. Similar properties are
worth close to $2 million in today's
money and the club felt they had
looked after their new recruit as best
they could.

After two weeks, however, the
Englishman strode into the Manly
president's office and told him he wasn't
happy with the accommodation.
Stunned but eager to sort the problem
out, the president asked what was
wrong with it. "The sea," Woodward
replied, "it's keeping me awake at night."

Party animals...

Rugby players love of their post-match entertainment is legendary and it's a brave (or stupid) man who tries to stand between a team and their beer once the final whistle blows.

BELOW Willie John McBride leads out the British Lions – 1974.

The British Lions team that toured South Africa in 1974 were certainly no exception and proved beyond doubt rugby players take their partying as seriously as they do their sport.

On one night of the tour, the manager of the hotel the team were staying at became so appalled by their drink-fuelled antics – including two of the party wandering naked through the corridors – that he threatened to call the local constabulary to break things up.

The threat, however, failed to move the Lions and their phlegmatic skipper, Willie John McBride, and the party continued. The police were duly called, arriving with dogs and vans ready to cart the tourists off to the clink. At this point McBride went calmly downstairs to the hotel's coffee machine, bought some milk and presented it to the police dogs.

They (quite literally) lapped it up, the police themselves were invited to join the party, they accepted and the party continued – much to the annoyance of the hotel manager.

Street football...

The great thing about rugby's miscreants and mischief makers is you can find them at every level of the game – from the local third XV all the way up to the top echelons of the sport.

This was famously proven in the aftermath of England's narrow Calcutta Cup victory over Scotland at Murrayfield in 1988 when opposing back row forwards Dean Richards and John Jeffrey decided to bury the hatchet and sample some of the delights of Edinburgh's night life.

Unfortunately they decided to take the Calcutta Cup with them and, after a few too many, decided to have an impromptu game of football in the street with the famous piece of silverware.

ABOVE Dean Richards – drunken football antics a million miles away!

Unsurprisingly the famous cup came off worst and the pair caused £1,000 worth of damage. The unfortunate and by now stone cold sober Jeffrey and Richards were quickly dealt with by their fuming unions – the former picking up a six-month ban, the latter an altogether more lenient one-match suspension.

Wags suggested they'd have to rename the silverware the Calcutta Shield after the pair's antics.

Home comforts...

Not everyone in the rugby fraternity is a big fan of the traditional post-match dinner, speeches and general pomp and ceremony.

BELOW Kitch Christie – not looking forward to any post-match speeches.

Certainly not World Cup-winning South African coach Kitch Christie, who made his feelings about the rituals that invariably follow a Test perfectly clear when he was called upon to make a speech in the wake of the Springboks' famous win over New Zealand in 1995.

Christie had been stuck in his chair for what seemed like hours and had had to listen to countless speeches when he was finally asked by the evening's master of ceremonies to give his own address to the assembled audience.

Quick as a flash, Christie rose to his feet and without a trace of irony, said: "Ladies and gentlemen, I am delighted to give you my address, which is number 14, West End Street, to which I hope quickly to return."

Initially the rest of the room had no idea what to make of Christie's joke, sitting in stunned silence before eventually giving him a long round of applause.

Flag day...

High jinks are part and parcel of a good tour but sometimes what seems like a good idea after a night on the tiles can appear altogether different in the cold light of morning. Just ask Ireland's Willie Anderson.

Anderson was invited to tour Argentina with the Penguins in 1980 and readily accepted the offer, hoping for some good rugby and some even better post-match entertainment. It was a decision he'd have plenty of time to regret.

Out in Argentina, the big forward duly went out for a few drinks with the some of the other players. At the end of the night, he spotted an Argentinian flag, taking an immediate fancy to it and 'liberated' it from its rightful place.

Unfortunately Anderson was caught in the act and rather than the anticipated severe talking to by the local police, he was thrown into jail. It was, after all, just a few years before the Falklands War and the Argentinians took a dim view of Anderson's perceived lack of respect for the national flag. It was to be months before the unfortunate Irishman was released.

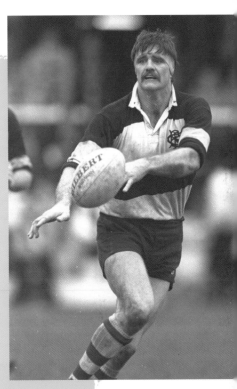

ABOVE Have you seen this man? Willie Anderson post 1980.

Room service...

Jealousy is an ugly emotion and it certainly caused all sorts of problems during the British Lions' visit to New Zealand in 1966 when the tourists were staying on the South Island.

The Lions were randomly split into two groups for their stay, the first group staying in the New Albion Hotel, the second at the less luxurious surroundings of the Old Albion nearby.

BELOW Lions legend Willie John McBride.

The split did not go down very well with two of the Old Albions guests – Irishmen Willie John McBride and Ronnie Lamont – and they decided to exact their revenge on their pampered team-mates at the New Albion.

Ensuring the rest of the squad was safely ensconced in the bar, McBride and Lamont crept into the New Albion and rifled through all the players' rooms, throwing playing kit and personal belongings alike out of the window and into the hotel garden before making their escape.

The next day the local papers were full of the stories of the incident and although the police investigated what was an embarrassing episode for the locals, the culprits were never discovered. In fact, none of the Lions themselves knew who did it until McBride revealed all in his 2004 autobiography.

Cadillac confusion...

Another tall tale illustrating the innate cheek of the Irish concerns the 1974 Lions tour of South Africa.

During the tour, the Lions left South Africa to fulfil a fixture in neighbouring Rhodesia (as it was then known) and after the game there was the obligatory post-match dinner and speeches. The ceremony was attended by the Rhodesian Prime Minister Ian Smith.

As the evening wore on two of the Lions – Irishmen Fergus Slattery and Dick Milliken – agreed they'd had enough and and decided to head back to the team hotel. The only problem was they had no transport and there were no taxis to be seen.

At this point, Slattery spotted an impressive looking Cadillac parked with black tinted windows parked outside and the duo decided they'd borrow the car for a quick spin.

After a few minutes driving around, the partition between the front seats and the back quietly slid down and a voice from the dark inquired: "Are you gentleman looking for a job?"

As Slattery and Milliken turned around, they realised the owner of the Cadillac was none other than the Rhodesian Prime Minister.

ABOVE Fergus Slattery – put that in your pipe and smoke it.

Musical madness...

The New Zealand team that toured the British Isles in 1993 were one of the strongest and most feared All Black sides to arrive on these shores and most pundits and fans fully expected them to return home unbeaten.

As it transpired, however, the Blacks were to be toppled on the tour when they were beaten 15-9 by England at Twickenham but it was what happened in the dressing rooms of HQ after the game that concerns us.

BELOW Don't Dream It's over... Well actually it was.

It's not often the New Zealanders lose to England and it was a dejected and disappointed group of players who trudged off the Twickenham pitch that day – only to be greeted by Kiwi pop star Neil Finn, the lead singer of Crowded House.

Finn had been watching the game from the stands and at the final whistle decided the Blacks would probably need cheering up a bit. Before the team knew what hit them, Finn launched into an unplugged medley of his greatest hits. What the players made of their uninvited guest remains a mystery.

Secret service...

Sir Clive Woodward may have been ridiculed after having the England meeting room swept for listening bugs during the 2003 World Cup but it was far from the first time that a spot of spying was on the agenda during the game's showpiece tournament.

Back in 1995 at the South African World Cup, England were drawn to face Australia in the quarter-finals and Will Carling's team were desperate to learn what tactics the Wallabies would employ for the crunch clash.

It was decided to dispatch the team psychologist Austin Swain to spy on an Australian training session. Swain cunningly disguised himself as a backpacker to get past security and duly picked up all the information that was required. In fact, his ruse was so successful that he even drank some of the beer laid on for the Australian management team.

"He returned having seen the whole training session," recalled Carling after the mission. "He told us which strike moves they were practising. It was all quite useful."

England fans will not need reminding Carling's team won the game 25-22.

ABOVE Will Carling relieved that a little bit of spying paid off.

Crime doesn't pay...

The players of Italian side Benetton Treviso probably weren't much looking forward to the mandatory press conference ahead of their league clash with Calvisano – until they spotted a purse snatcher and gave chase.

The unfortunate thief grabbed a purse near the team's hotel and probably thought he had got away with his crime until he noticed Benetton lock Andrea Gritti and winger Massimiliano Perziano, both Italian internationals, in hot pursuit of him.

BELOW Benetton Treviso practising thier crime caper moves.

Understandably terrified at the prospect of being collared by the two burly stars, the thief promptly made a run for it and tried to hide in a nearby nursery school. But the Benetton pair were not going to be thrown off the scent that easily and cornered their man at the school until the local police arrived and arrested him.

Rumour has it the thief wept with relief when the police turned up – preferring to face the wrath of the law rather than the two angry rugby players.

COACH ON THE PITCH

COACHES TACTICS

FANTASTIC FANS

A TRIBUTE TO THOSE WHO CHEER FROM THE SIDELINES

Chapter 5

Without the fans, rugby would sadly be an altogether quieter affair without the colour, wit and cacophony of noise that make matches from Bath to Brisbane and Wellington to Wakefield such unmissable moments for spectators of all ages.

Rugby supporters are rightly renowned for their sense of humour (unless, of course, the club bar runs dry) and it is an enduring testimony to the spirit in which the game is still played that your average fan thinks segregation is probably a religious cult.

In this chapter, we bring you some hilarious tales of fans and their foibles from every corner of the rugby-playing world, including the story of how a Scotland supporter and his sporran caused a major security alert and the New Zealand woman who decided to take the law into her own hands when the French came to town.

And, of course, there's a healthy selection of some of the best supporter-themed jokes on the planet, which prove beyond doubt that all rugby fans live to laugh at someone else's expense.

Ugly duckling...

Wallaby legend David Campese could delight and annoy in equal measure and even his Australian team-mates happily admit the outspoken winger fancied himself off the pitch just much as he did on it.

BELOW Campo – ladies man?

But one story (not told by the man himself, incidentally) proves that Campo was not quite as irresistible to the ladies as he would have liked to think.

The year was 1992, just 12 months after Australia's World Cup final win over England at Twickenham, and Campo was at a music festival with fellow Wallaby Michael Lynagh when they noticed a group of rather attractive girls looking in their direction and whispering furiously.

Campo knew the girls were trying to decide whether it was him or not and moved closer so he could overhear their breathless debate.

What he actually heard was one of the them admitting: "I've never been so disappointed in all my life. He's nowhere as good looking in real life as he is on television."

Bare-faced cheek...

Perhaps the most famous rugby 'fan' of them all is Erica Roe, who earned her place in folklore when she decided to streak across the hallowed Twickenham turf during half-time of England's 1982 clash with the Wallabies.

Pictures of Miss Roe were splashed all over the newspapers the following day but what wasn't reported at the time was the reaction of the England players to her impromptu pitch invasion.

England were captained by Bill Beaumont at the time and it was in the days when teams stayed out during the half-time break rather than retreating to warmth of the dressing room.

ABOVE Erica Roe being escorted from the premises.

As Beaumont was attempting to rally his troops, he noticed their attention to what he was saying was not exactly total.

They were all ogling Miss Roe, who was doing her stuff behind Beaumont's back. Exasperated, the captain demanded to know what the problem was, to which one of the players, Steve Smith, quickly replied: 'It's because there's a girl running around over there with your bum on her chest' – a reference to Beaumont's legendarily large behind.

Roe's streak obviously did not distract too greatly though as Beaumont's side wrapped up a 15-11 win in the second-half.

Black and white...

Like any sport, rugby would be nothing without the fans and there are many examples where the intervention of supporters has saved a game from an embarrassing and premature end.

BELOW Uganda playing France in 2004 in a slightly more traditional colour scheme.

Take the example of the 1935 clash between Uganda and Kenya in Entebbe, which appeared doomed before a ball had been kicked or a body rucked as both sides turned up wearing white shirts.

Neither side had any spare kit and the referee insisted he could not take control of a match with 30 players all decked out in the same shirts.

Luckily, however, there was one quick-thinking female fan in the crowd who produced a bottle of black dye and once an iron bath had been found, promptly dyed the Ugandan shirts. The African sun did the rest and the game was finally played.

Heaven sent...

Rugby fans are a constant source of oval-shaped jokes, as this example proves...

A diehard Welsh rugby fan is on his way home from the pub after celebrating Wales' Grand Slam when he is tragically knocked by a runaway lorry and killed instantly.

When he arrives at Heaven's pearly gates, he's met by St Peter, who asks him to wait while he checks his credentials. St Peter soon returns and tells the Welsh fan he cannot enter the kingdom of Heaven because he'd spent his money on beer and fast women and had failed to live a virtuous life.

To make matters worse, the supporter is told he'll have go to Hell immediately and is shown to an escalator that leads all the way down to the everlasting fires of the Devil's den.

ABOVE A Welshman's idea of hell as Jonny Wilkinson sends that kick on its way.

At the bottom of the escalator there's a set of double doors, which he pushes open nervously and is suddenly blinded by a shining light.

When he gets his bearings, he realises he's in the Millennium Stadium surrounded by thousands of fellow Welsh fans. At one end of the ground there's a massive television screen, flashing the message 'Next showing starts in four minutes'. At this point the fan is convinced he's been sent to Heaven by mistake, until the man next to him leans over and days: "Don't get too excited, it's the 2003 World Cup final."

Champagne rugby...

BELOW Avril Malan, Springbok captain during the 1960/61 Tour.

The 1960-61 Springbok team that toured Britain were what you'd call a formidable bunch and their burly, abrasive forwards in particular were not to be taken lightly.

In the Test match against Scotland at Murrayfield the South African pack were giving the home eight such a torrid afternoon – they won seven strikes against the head – that even the most ardent Scottish fans in the crowd knew the writing was one the wall for their boys.

Leading the way was Springbok hooker Abie Malan who was in the thick of all the action. At one line-out in the second-half, with the result for the tourists already in the bag, Malan picked up the ball and prepared to throw in, bellowing out a coded call of "Nineteen twenty six" to his jumpers.

"Jesus," replied one waggish Scottish fan from the stands, "they're ordering the champagne already."

Lady lout...

Some supporters are happy to leave the violence to the players out on the pitch. Some, however, are not.

During a particularly vicious encounter between South Canterbury and the touring French side in the early 60s, one female fan was getting increasingly frustrated with the visitors' rough house tactics.

She finally snapped when Tricolores skipper Michel Crauste laid out one of the Canterbury players with a blatant high tackle, running out onto the pitch to give Crauste a piece of her mind.

But not content with her verbal volley, she then decided to punch the bemused Frenchman on the back of the neck before she was unceremoniously escorted off the pitch by the police.

"I was so mad I did not know what I was doing," confessed the 56-year-old woman after the game. "I hit him hard, but I don't think it hurt. I think he got a bit of a shock though."

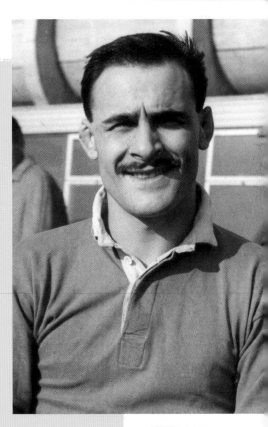

ABOVE Michel Crauste in happier days.

Lashing down...

A classic rugby joke that proves there's never any love lost between the Home Nations.

A Welsh fan, an Irish fan and an English fan are all arrested in Saudi Arabia after being caught red-handed with a crate of contraband booze and are thrown into the local jail.

After months languishing in prison, the men are finally sentenced to 20 lashes before they are set free. All three are terrified by the painful prospect until the local Sheikh unexpectedly turns up and tells them that in honour of his wife's birthday, they can each have one wish before they are whipped.

The Welsh fans thinks long and hard and decides he's like a pillow strapped to his back before he is lashed. The Sheikh obliges but the pillow only lasts for 10 lashes and the Welshman is carried off bleeding and crying.

Next is the Englishman and with a smug smile he asks the benevolent Sheikh if he can have two pillows strapped to his back. The Sheikh agrees and the Englishman gets little more than a few scratches on his back after his punishment, walking away with a big grin.

Finally it's the Irishman's turn. He strides forward confidently and tells the Sheikh that rather than the 20 lashes he has been sentenced to, he would like to have a 100. The Sheikh is understandably stunned but also rather impressed and asks the Irishman what he would like to have strapped to his back before his dreadful beating. "The Englishman," he replies.

Ball boy...

The noise of the fans cheering or jeering from the sidelines can inspire or intimidate players in equal measure but it is a completely different story when the fans, however good natured, actually spill out onto the pitch.

Just ask Paul Burke. During the 1999-2000 season Burke was playing for Cardiff against arch-rivals Newport at the Arm's Park. With the match heading quickly to full-time, Cardiff had just scored a try in the corner to level the scores and Burke was faced with a difficult conversion to win the local derby.

Just as he prepared for the all-important kick, a drunken supporter appeared as if from nowhere, sprinted across the pitch and belted Burke's lovingly-placed ball high into the stands.

As so often in these situations, the errant fan was duly tackled to the floor by the local constabulary's finest and Burke had to go through the anxiety-inducing ordeal all over again. To his credit, he held his nerve and slotted the conversion.

"I don't comment whenever there's controversy," Burke diplomatically said after the game. "I've always believed that's it's better to keep your mouth shut and appear stupid than to open it and remove all doubt."

ABOVE Paul Burke looking for his ball.

Taxi for tony...

The wit of your average rugby fan is beyond question but certain anonymous individuals have taken the art of grandstand humour to new levels.

BELOW Tony O'Reilly rushing to his car.

One supporter in this category was certainly in the Twickenham crowd for the 1970 meeting between England and Ireland.

The match is famous for the last-minute recall of Irish legend Tony O'Reilly, who hadn't played for his country for seven years but was hastily drafted into the team after an injury. By now O'Reilly was a successful businessman and caused quite a stir in the newspapers when he arrived for training on the eve of the game in a chauffeur-driven Rolls Royce.

Come matchday and O'Reilly was immediately targeted by England, who hoped he would prove the weak link. Early in the first-half he was tested by a high ball which he took – at about the same time as the eight English forwards descended on him en masse.

As O'Reilly gingerly picked himself, the Twickenham crowd went silent. Silent, that is, until a lone Irish voice rang out: "And you can kick his f*****g chauffeur, too!"

Centre of attention...

Former England star Jeremy Guscott enjoyed a distinguished Test career for England and the Lions that spanned a decade. Unlike any of his front row team-mates, however, he also managed to turn a few female heads in the process. In fact, the dashing centre even landed himself the odd modelling contract, such were his unblemished good looks and he was the constant source of pretty boy jokes for his Bath and England colleagues.

Guscott finally retired from international rugby after the 1999 World Cup but he still found himself in great demand as an after-dinner speaker at various charity functions.

At one particular event, Guscott delivered one of his speeches, regaling the crowd with various behind-the-scenes anecdotes from his illustrious career.

When he had finished, the master of ceremonies for the evening stepped in and asked the audience if anyone had any questions for their guest speaker. There was an embarrassing pause before a female voice chimed out from the back of the room. "Is he married?"

ABOVE Jeremy Guscott is his Bath playing days – a model of a player.

Furry friend...

Rugby supporters often travel thousands of miles to cheer on their side but in the case of one Scottish fan, his journey to Australia in 2003 for the World Cup was very nearly a wasted one.

The fan, 36-year-old Edinburgh man Torquil Fitch, was stopped at Brisbane Airport by the authorities when they searched his luggage and found an "unidentifiable' furry object in one of his bags, prompting a huge security scare.

The only problem was the offending item was nothing more dangerous than Fitch's sporran, which he planned to wear with his kilt at Scotland's upcoming games.

BELOW Scottish fans entertain the crowd!

"They had clearly never encountered anything quite like it before and were obviously genuinely concerned," Fitch said after being interrogated. "Once I had explained the position thoroughly and they were satisfied my sporran presented no threat to the flora and fauna of Australia, the anxiety disappeared. There was even some good-natured banter among the officials with one of them suggesting it was along the same lines as 'koala road kill!'"

Finch later told reporters that the sporran was actually known as Fred.

Cut off point...

Some rugby fans are passionate are about their club or country and will go to virtually any lengths to show their diehard support. Some, however, are just plain fanatical.

Take the eye-watering case of the Welshman who went to such extremes to show his dedication to

Welsh supporters in good cheer.

the Wales team that he ended up in hospital minus a rather part important part of his anatomy.

The man in question was watching Wales take on England in a Six Nations clash in the Leigh Social Club in Caerphilly when he announced to everyone in the bar that he'd cut his own testicles off if Wales managed to pull off an unlikely win over the English.

Unfortunately, that's exactly what did happen and the man duly disappeared outside for a few moments, returning later with blood splattered everywhere and, yes, his own testicles in his hand to show off to fellow drinkers.

An ambulance was quickly called and the man, who was on medication and had been drinking heavily throughout the afternoon, was rushed off to the nearest hospital.

Getting personal...

Thousands of New Zealand rugby fans were desperate to get hold of tickets for the final of the 1987 World Cup between the All Blacks and France.

In fact, so desperate that it came as little surprise to anyone when the following personal ad placed by a cheeky fan appeared in a Kiwi newspaper days before the big match.

'Young rugby supporter of good appearance and sound health offers hand in marriage to any young lady with two tickets for the World Cup final. Please send photograph of the tickets'.

BELOW New Zealand
supporters lucky
enough to be at a game.

The 1877 West Wales Challenge Cup final between Cardiff and Llanelli had to be abandoned after a light-fingered spectator scarpered with the match ball. No replacement could be found and the referee had no choice but to call off the game.

Swapping shirts...

The old ones are the best, as proven by this classic piece of rugby humour...

A family of English rugby fans are out on a shopping trip together. They decide to go to a sports shop when the 10-year-old son suddenly announces to his sister that he wants to be a Wales supporter and he's going to buy a Welsh shirt to prove the point.

"What do you want to do that for," his stunned sister asks.
"They've just won the Grand Slam and I like the way they play the game," he replies. His sister takes this all in and then whacks him over the back of the head, telling him to go and talk to his mum.

Off goes the lad with the Welsh jersey in his hand and finds his mum. "Mum, I've decided I'm going to be a Wales supporter and would like this jersey for Christmas."

The mother is obviously outraged and she too whacks him about the head, sending him over to the face the wrath of his father. "Dad, I've decided I'm going to be a Wales supporter and would like this jersey for Christmas." The father is furious and promptly whacks the boy's head, screaming at him that no child of his will ever support Wales.

On the way home, the father begins to calm down a bit and asks his son whether he's learnt anything from what happened in the shop.
"Yes," comes the defiant reply. "I've only been a Wales fan for an hour but I've already learnt to hate you English bastards."

Death becomes her...

A fervent Scotland fan is in Edinburgh to see his side take on the English for the Calcutta Cup. The game has been sold out for months and Murrayfield is packed to the rafters with Scots desperate to see the auld enemy sent packing.

The thing is, there's an empty seat right next to the fan. It's the only free space in the whole stadium and with just two minutes to go before the big kick-off, a man in the row behind leans forward and taps the guy on the shoulder.

"Excuse me, why isn't there anyone sitting there? There's people who would kill for that seat." "I bought the other ticket for my wife," comes the reply. "Where is she?"

By now the man has his tears in his eyes. "She died recently in a car crash." "I'm very sorry," says the chap behind. "So, you're keeping her seat vacant as a mark of respect then?" "No, I offered the ticket to all my family." "Really and no-one wanted it? "No, none of my friends fancied it either." "Unbelievable." "I know, they all wanted to go to the funeral."

GOOSE

GRUDGE MATCH

FACTS AND FIGURES
A TRAWL THROUGH RUGBY'S ARCHIVES

Records, as someone almost once said, are there to be broken. And we're not talking about a drunken rampage through HMV.

The history of rugby, like any other sport, is a treasure trove of milestones and landmarks, firsts and lasts and here we present the quirkiest and most essential information for any self-respecting fan or player who needs to know how to talk the talk in the bar after the game.

So if you want to know who is the most expensive signing in the professional era, why the All Blacks lost two Test matches on the same day or why the Americans have an unusual claim to Olympic rugby fame, this chapter has got the lot.

So if you've got absolutely no idea why Irish rugby celebrated its centenary twice (and oh, it wasn't just a good excuse for another Guinness) or how the unfortunately-named Tommy Vile made Five Nations history, then prepare to be enlightened.

England's home...

Twickenham will celebrate a century of staging international rugby in 2010. The first Test played at the famous ground was England versus Wales in January 1910, which the home side fittingly won 11-6.

The first game ever at HQ, however, was a club clash between London rivals Harlequins and Richmond in 1909. The first team to record a victory at Twickenham were the touring Springboks, who beat England 9-3 in 1913. The oldest ground in international rugby, however, is Lansdowne Road, which saw its first Test in February 1884 when Ireland took on England.

BELOW England celebrate winning the Calcutta Cup at Twickenham.

Former England prop Jason Leonard is the most-capped player in rugby history. The Harlequins front row forward made his international debut in 1990 against Argentina and won a total of 114 caps before finally announcing his retirement. He captained the team twice but scored just one try for his country.

Different balls...

Welsh legend JPR Williams will forever be remembered as one of the true greats of the game but it could have been a very different story if the abrasive full-back with the unmistakable sideburns had not turned his back on tennis in favour of the oval ball. Three years before he made his Wales debut in 1969, Williams won the Wimbledon Junior Boys title but thankfully opted to concentrate on rugby rather than tennis.

Lawrence Dallaglio was one of England's finest ever forwards but it could have been a different story if the Wasps number eight had decided to turn his back on the country of his birth. Lots of people know Dallaglio has an Italian father but what is less well documented are his mother's Irish connections – which led to a call from the Irish Rugby Union in 1994 inquiring whether the future World Cup winner would like to play for Ireland. Thankfully for English fans, Dallaglio declined the invitation.

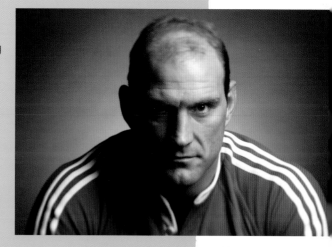

ABOVE Lawrence Dallaglio who could have played for the Irish or Italian teams.

Radio waves...

Rugby entered the communication age in 1926 when live radio commentary of a game in New Zealand was broadcast. The match between Christchurch and High School Old Boys was the first ever to be covered by radio. Television got in on the act 12 years later when the few people who owned sets were able to watch pictures of England's clash with Scotland at Twickenham.

Tough-as-teak All Black prop Steve McDowell was also a leading judo exponent and was selected to represent New Zealand at the 1980 Olympic Games in Moscow. Unfortunately for McDowell, New Zealand were one of the countries who decided to boycott the Games and his dreams of gold disappeared.

BELOW Steve McDowell leads the All Blacks in the 'Haka'.

Shea class...

A 'full house' is when a player scores a try, a conversion, a drop goal and a penalty in the same game and the first man to achieve that in international rugby was Jerry Shea of Wales. Shea pulled off his 'full house' in January 1920 as Wales beat England at Swansea.

There are a few examples of father and sons playing against each other but as far the records show, there is only one case of a father and son with the same name doing so. The two men in question were (both) George Nepia, who lined up against each other for Poverty Bay and Olympians respectively in New Zealand in 1950. Incidentally, the two men both played full-back. And it was a case of age before beauty with George senior, who was 45-years-old and a former All Black, emerging victorious with his Poverty bay team.

ABOVE New Zealand sensation George Nepia snr.

Tunnel vision ...

Playing Australia is always a daunting prospect, especially when you've only got 14 men on the pitch as England did against the Wallabies at Twickenham in 1984. Hooker Steve Mills had to come off injured but his replacement, Steve Brain, left his team shorthanded for 13 long minutes because the doors between the tunnel and the pitch were locked and he couldn't get out.

BELOW Tom Voyce being tackled by a Worcester player.

The fastest ever try in the history of the then Five Nations came in 1999 when Scotland's John Leslie touched down after just 10.8 seconds against Wales at Murrayfield. The Scots went on to win 33-20. However, the distinction of scoring the fastest try in British rugby history belongs to Wasps winger Tom Voyce, who raced over after an incredible 9.63 seconds in a 2004 Premiership clash with Harlequins.

Perfect ten...

Most players would be delighted to score a hat-trick of tries but Ashley Billington had other ideas when Hong Kong met Singapore in a World Cup qualifier in 1994.
Not content with his first-half hat-trick, Billington went on to score a record total of 10 tries.

Although America can hardly claim to being a hotbed of rugby, the States can lay claim to be being the reigning Olympic champions. The Eagles side, featuring many players from Stanford University, won gold at the 1924 Games in Paris after beating France in the final and since rugby disappeared from the Olympic schedule four years later when the Games were held in Amsterdam, America remain Olympic champions.

ABOVE The Devonport Services stand by as the 1924 USA Olympic Rugby Team give their war cry before a match at Plymouth.

Double celebration...

The Irish Rugby Union celebrated its centenary in 1974 – and then again in 1979. The reason? When the IRU was originally set up in Dublin in 1874, the assembled administrators eventually realised than no-one from Ulster had been invited, so they went through the whole procedure again five years later. Hence the two celebrations.

Bath became the first club side in league history to field a side with 15 full internationals in September 1998 when they played Gloucester at the Recreation Ground. Thankfully for the Bath faithful, their star-studded side emerged narrow 21-16 winners.

ABOVE Zak Feau'nati heads up the pack for Bath.

Long haul...

The 1888 British Lions that toured New Zealand and Australia were nothing if not durable. The squad featured a mere 22 players, they were away from home for 35 weeks and three days and they played an energy-sapping 35 matches in total. Incredibly, a Swinton player called H Eagles featured in all 35 games for the tourists.

Welshman James Griffiths had an international debut to forget when he won his first cap against Samoa in 2000. In what was a predictably bruising encounter against the South Sea Islanders, Griffiths was summoned from the bench in the second-half and lasted a full 60 seconds on the pitch before he was sin-binned.

ABOVE The British Lions tour, a hundred years on.

Historic first...

The British Lions may represent the cream of northern hemisphere rugby but the famous tourists were actually created by a group of cricketers. In 1888, a cricket team were touring Australia when they hit on the idea of replicating the trip with a group of rugby players. A.E. Stoddart was approached to lead the side and although the RFU refused to recognise the idea, a tour of the southern colonies was organised and the Lions were born.

The first ever rugby international took place in 1871 between Scotland and England. The historic game was played at Raeburn Place in Edinburgh and saw the home side emerge as the victors by a goal and a try to England's solitary goal. It was certainly a crowded fixture as the game was played in the era when teams still consisted of 20 players. It was to be six more years before teams were reduced to 15 per side.

BELOW The first ever international in 1871 took place between these English and Scottish teams.

Divine intervention...

Whether God is a rugby fan is debatable but judging by his divine intervention during the USA's clash with France in 1991, the evidence points to not. With the French leading 10-3 minutes after the break in Colorado, the match had to be abandoned – because the scoreboard was struck by lightning.

The Varsity match between Oxford and Cambridge universities was first played in 1872. The first fixture was played in Oxford and the following year Cambridge acted as hosts. The 1874 game and all subsequent meetings have been played in London.

Australia		England
1	Tries	1
0	Conversions	0
4	Penalties	4
0	Drop Goals	1
17	Score	20

Extra Time

ABOVE Thankfully this scoreboard wasn't struck by lightning.

Record romp...

Few would disagree that the inception of leagues in the English game in 1987 has raised standards but there was certainly no evidence of this improvement in 1999 when Richmond met Bedford in a top-flight clash. The Londoners walloped Bedford 106-12, running in 16 tries in the process, to set a league record that stands to this day.

BELOW The Bedford team of 1998 a year before their Richmond drubbing.

New Zealand are the only rugby-playing country to have played two full Test matches on the same day. The unique incident came in September 1949 when an All Blacks side took on Australia in Wellington while another New Zealand XV played South Africa in Durban. It was far from a successful experiment however – the first team losing 11-6 to the Wallabies, their counterparts thousands of miles away going down 9-3 to the Springboks.

Senior citizen...

The oldest rugby club in the world is Cambridge University, which was founded in 1839 by a student called Arthur Peel. The Sydney University Club in Australia was the first to be established outside Britain and Ireland when it was formed in 1864.

Modern Test match rugby players may be getting younger and younger but the record for the youngest player ever to appear in the Championship still belongs to Frank Hewitt, who was just 17 years and 157 days old when he played for Ireland in 1924.

ABOVE The Cambridge XV rugby team – 1874.

The oldest player to appear in the tournament did so three years earlier. His name was Tommy Vile and he was a stately 38 years and 152 days young when he was picked for Wales.

Slippery customer...

Australia are known as the Wallabies but on their 1908 tour to Great Britain, the tourists actually brought a live snake with them as the team mascot. Sadly, the British weather didn't agree with the snake and it died just hours before the Australians lost their first game of the tour to Llanelli.

BELOW The French win a lineout at the Stade De France against Wales.

France are a perennial Championship power these days but the Tricolores were not always a force to be reckoned with. The French were admitted to the tournament in 1910 but won just one game – a one-point victory against Scotland – in the next four campaigns. They failed to win a single match though between 1931 and 1947 because they were kicked out of the competition by the Home Nations after allegations French clubs were flouting the game's amateur ethos and paying their players.

Fleeting fame...

Many players have had the misfortune to be playing at the same time, and in the same position, as some of the game's true greats but few could claim to be as unlucky as Maesteg scrum-half Chico Hopkins. A fine number nine in his own right, Hopkins had the great handicap of trying to force his way into the Wales team at the same time as the legendary Gareth Edwards. As a result, Hopkins spent most of his international 'career' on the bench. Until, that is, Wales were playing England in 1970 and Edwards had to come off with an injury. Hopkins moment had finally come and with his side trailing by seven points and 15 minutes left on the clock, he made the

ABOVE The last person you'd want to be behind in the pecking order — Gareth Edwards.

most dramatic of impacts – scoring the try which gave Wales a famous 17-13 win. Sadly for the Maesteg man, his contribution was not enough to earn him another game in the Welsh colours and his 15 minutes of fame against England was to be his first and last taste of international rugby.

Floodlights made their first impression on rugby as far back as 1878 when Broughton and Swinton made history by playing a fixture under artificial illumination.

Colour blind...

The first-ever Test between the All Blacks and the Lions in Christchurch in 1930 would have confused the modern fan because New Zealand actually played the game in white shirts and the tourists in dark blue.

Jonny Wilkinson has smashed countless records since his England debut in 1998 but it is the speed of his exploits that is most striking. Before Wilkinson, Rob Andrew held the record as England's leading all-time points scorer with 396, a mark that the younger man eclipsed in 2001 as England smashed the French 48-19 at Twickenham. Andrew played 70 Tests over 12 years to set his mark. In contrast, Wilkinson needed just three seasons and a mere 27 matches to overtake his predecessor in the England number ten shirt.

Dynamic davies...

England have produced many fine captains over the years but in terms of winning percentages, the most successful ever is William 'Dave' Davies. He captained England 11 times from 1921 and his record of won 10, drawn one, makes his statistically more successful than any other England skipper. Bizarrely, Davies was actually born in Wales.

In the days before cheap and easy air travel, tours could be long and arduous affairs, particularly if teams had to travel great

ABOVE The England team from 1921.

distances by boat. It was the All Blacks who broke the mould when they became the first rugby team to travel by air in 1947, chartering a flying boat to take the squad to Australia.

Glorious gavin...

Gavin Hastings holds the record for the most points in Test matches for the British Lions. The big Scottish full-back amassed 66 points on the 1989 tour to Australia and the trip to New Zealand four years later. Legendary Irishman Willie John McBride holds the distinction of the most Lions caps with a staggering 17 between 1962 and 1974.

BELOW Gavin Hastings in action for The Lions.

The 1973 Five Nations was one of the most curious in the long history of the tournament. After the teams had played their four fixtures, each country boasted a record of won two, lost two, resulting in an unique five-way tie for the title. It was still an improvement on the competition the previous year, however, which had to be abandoned because Scotland and Wales refused to play in Ireland because of the troubles.

World cup landmark...

New Zealand flanker Michael Jones will forever be remembered in the record books as the first player ever to score a try at a World Cup. The dynamic All Black forward touched down against Italy in the opening game of the 1987 finals to guarantee his own little slice of rugby immortality. Another former All Black, Va'aiga Tuigamala, holds another try-scoring distinction. His score for the Blacks against the Wallabies in 1992 was the first-ever 'five pointer' in the history of the game after the authorities decided to try and encourage a more adventurous style of play.

Former Wales fly-half Neil Jenkins became the first play in international rugby history to pass the 1,000 point barrier in 2001 when England visited the Millennium Stadium. Unfortunately for Jenkins, Wales were beaten 44-15.

ABOVE Neil Jenkins playing for The British Lions.

Title race...

Wales long-awaited 2005 Grand Slam took their total of Championship titles to 34 — just one short of England's record haul of 35. Scotland and France are tied on 22 (despite the fact the Tricolores only gained admission to the tournament in 1910), while Ireland have 18. Italy, admitted to the expanded Six Nations in 200, are yet to open their account. England also lead the Grand Slam list with 12. Wales have nine, France nine, Scotland three and Ireland one solitary clean sweep.

BELOW Wales on their way to the Grand Slam assisted by Gavin Henson.

In the modern era there are many examples of players who have represented more than one country but James Marsh still remains the only man to have turned out for two different teams in the Championship. A doctor by trade, Marsh played for Scotland in the 1889 season before moving to Manchester. Three years later he turned out in the white of England. But despite his shifting allegiances, Marsh still only won three caps in total (two for Scotland, one for England) and tow of them were against Ireland.

Bench mark...

Tactical substitutions and impact players are part and parcel of the modern game but it is not that long ago that replacements (for injury or any other reason) were still unheard of. Even into the early 1960s, coaches were not allowed to bring anyone else onto the field if a player was injured and the game's first-ever substitution did not happen until 1968. The match in question was the Lions first game of their South African tour against Western Transvaal and the historic change occurred when Irishman Mike Gibson was injured – paving the way for compatriot Barry Bresnihan to make a little bit of rugby history.

ABOVE Va'aiga Tuigamala – how much?

When rugby went professional in 1995 in the wake of the World Cup in South Africa, players suddenly realised they could be transfered between clubs. However, the price of these transfers has decreased rather than risen over the intervening years and the £1 million Newcastle Falcons paid Wigan rugby league side in 1997 to secure the services of Va'aiga Tuigamala remains a world record fee for the sport.

Trivia for fans...

BELOW Hugo Porta preparing to drop goal.

James Bevan became the first player to captain Wales in an international game in 1881 when he led his side out to face England at Blackheath. What is less well known is the fact Bevan was actually born in Brisbane in Australia.

The last recorded instance of a 0-0 scoreline at international level was in 1964 when Scotland and New Zealand failed to conjure up a single point between them at Murrayfield.

The Tri-Nations tournament between New Zealand, Australia and South Africa began life in 1996 and saw the All Blacks crowned champions. New Zealand have landed the title five times in total while the Wallabies and the Springboks can boast two triumphs apiece.

PLAYERS IN THE BAR

The pictures in this book were provided courtesy of the following:
Getty Images
101 Bayham Street, London, NW1 0AG

The Cartoons in this book were provided courtesy of:
Steve Gammond and Pete Neame

Book design and artwork by Kevin Gardner,
based on an original design by Nicole Saward

Published by Green Umbrella

Series Editors Jules Gammond, Tim Exell, Vanessa Gardner

Compiled and Written by Iain Spragg

BIBLIOGRAPHY

'Outrageous Rugby Moments' Keith Quinn – *Hodder Moa Beckett Publishing (2002)*
'Rugby Union Fact Book' Chris Rhys – *Guinness Publishing (1992)*
'Odd–Shaped Balls' John Scally – *Mainstream Publishing (2004)*
'Rugby And All That' Martin Johnson – *Hodder and Stoughton (2000)*
'Beaumont's Up And Under' with Mark Baldwin – *Sanctuary Publishing (2005)*
'Ruck 'n' Muck' Iain Spragg – *WHSmith Limited (2003)*
'Classic Rugby Clangers' David Mortimer – *Robson Books (2003)*
'Sports 'n' All' Tim Forrester – *Chameleon Books (1997)*
'The International Rugby Almanack' edited by Derek Wyatt – *Blandford Books (1995)*
'Rugby's Strangest Matches' John Griffiths – *Robson Books (2000)*